A Taste of Satisfaction

Becoming Satisfied with
the Bread of Life...

Day by Day
for 31 Days

by

Kay Harms

Melinda,
Taste and
see that the
Lord is truly
satisfying!
Ps. 66:16
Kay

Off the Beaten Path Ministries

First published by Lulu 10/30/2011

ISBN #: 978-1-105-20061-8

To order additional copies of this resource, contact *Off the Beaten Path Ministries* at offthebeatenpathministries.com

Printed in the United States of America

To my parents, Jerry and Louise...

When I count my blessings and name them one by one, you are always at the top of the list. I can think of no greater blessing than to be raised in a home where Jesus Christ is loved, honored, and obeyed.

You have both demonstrated to me throughout the years that our God can indeed satisfy our every need. You have proven this simple truth through your faithfulness to the practice of tithing, your consistency in going to the house of the Lord each Sunday for worship, your allegiance to the Bible and its pattern for living, and your devoted service to others. I can only assume you have been able to give freely and generously because you are satisfied with the provision of God.

But perhaps the greatest demonstration you have given to me of God's faithfulness is your simple contentment. Instead of complaining, striving with God, or seeking the pursuits of this world, you have shown me and the rest of our family what it means to live richly satisfied lives at the generous hand of our Lord. I have been blessed by your satisfied lives.

Acknowledgements

I would like to express my deepest appreciation to those who have encouraged and assisted me as I penned this simple devotional book. Trust me. I do not take lightly the task of interpreting God's Word for such a book that is meant to be used in a person's quiet time. So the people who stayed on me to press on with this daunting task were integral to its completion.

Thank you, Kim Tucker, for reading every entry, looking up every scripture, and answering every question. The readers have you to thank for trimming down the number of additional scriptures listed each day to a manageable, enjoyable and ultimately satisfying number. Thank you for insisting that I consider their time limitations. I am sure they will appreciate your diligence.

And thank you, Mother (Louise Winton), for editing my work. Actually, you not only corrected my grammar, punctuation, sentence construction and word choice mistakes, but you kept me from making many such errors to begin with. I learned to diagram sentences at your chalk board well before I was supposed to and hopefully you reaped the fruit of that investment as you read over my manuscript with a keen eye. I am so grateful to you for teaching me well and for correcting me when I somehow missed what you had taught.

Lastly, thank you, my dear family, for all your support. James, Daniel, and Abigail, you are the blessings God most often uses to lift my spirits, anchor my feet, and give wind to my dreams. I love you so very much.

Come and Taste!

At first it might seem a little selfish and self-centered to use a devotional guide that helps you find personal satisfaction. Wouldn't it be nobler to go through a devotional book about praising God, sharing the gospel, serving others, or glorifying Him? I would agree with that premise except for three undeniable factors.

First of all, I think God makes it very clear He wants us to have satisfied souls. He promises over and over in His Word to *satisfy* His children. He undoubtedly created us with needy, hungry souls so that, as a baby latches on to its mother for physical nourishment, we would cry out for our Father, seek all we desire from Him, and stick close to Him, our one true source for soul satisfaction.

Secondly, I have found that when my soul is famished and I am not full of the unconditional love, significance, purpose, joy, security, and intimacy I so desperately crave, I am less prone and harder pressed to glorify God, praise Him, serve Him, minister to others, or share the gospel. But when I have drawn close to Him, drunk fully from His living water and eaten steadily from the Bread of Life, I am indeed able and even anxious to do those very things. Just as Jesus promised the Samaritan woman at the well in John 4, His living water flows through me like a steady river and bubbles up, splashing freely on those around me. When I have a satisfied soul, I will supernaturally love, give, and be gracious. And I will not resent those who need such things from me.

Finally, we are invited by God Himself to "taste and see that the Lord is good." He has beckoned us to His table, but so few of us have pulled up a chair, put our napkins in our laps, and partaken of His divine satisfaction.

A Journey of Satisfaction through God's Word

Throughout the Word of God, the theme of soul satisfaction makes a prevalent appearance. God placed Adam and Eve in a richly satisfying garden and gave them ample beauty, food, and resources to satisfy their every need. Most importantly, they had His very presence and perfect fellowship. He completely satisfied this first couple…until they turned to something else that looked fulfilling, but turned out to be disappointing.

Later, He brought His chosen people out of Egypt in order to release them from their captivity, but also so He could take them to a land flowing with milk and honey, a land where He would satisfy them in ways their task masters never could. On the way there, He taught them through a steady diet of manna—bread from heaven—to look only to Him for satisfaction. The exodus is a picture of salvation and satisfaction, the very things God offers us even today.

David and others wrote in Psalms about how our souls thirst and hunger for that which the world cannot provide and how God satisfies our yearning souls completely. The psalmists used the imagery of tasty, nourishing, and satisfying food to communicate how well God's presence, provision, and Word fill our hungry souls. Consider the following outtakes.

O God, Though art my God;
I shall seek Thee earnestly;
My soul thirsts for Thee,
My flesh yearns for Thee,
In a dry and weary land where there is no water.
(Psalm 63:1)

Lord, all my desire is before Thee;
And my sighing is not hidden from Thee.
(Psalm 38:9)

O taste and see that the Lord is good;
How blessed is the man who takes refuge in Him!
(Psalm 34:8)

My soul is satisfied as with marrow and fatness,
And my mouth offers praises with joyful lips.
(Psalm 63:5)

Let them give thanks to the Lord for His lovingkindness,
And for His wonders to the sons of men!
For He has satisfied the thirsty soul,
And the hungry soul He has filled with what is good.
(Psalm 107:8-9)

Return to your rest, O my soul,
For the Lord has dealt bountifully with you.
(Psalm 116:7)

Come and hear, all who fear God,
And I will tell of what He has done for my soul.
(Psalm 66:16)

In the books of Isaiah and Jeremiah, God addresses the fact that His people have forsaken Him, the "fountain of living waters," to hew for themselves broken cisterns that cannot satisfy their souls. He urges them, and us, to return to Him so we can "eat what is good and delight…in abundance." He promises to feed our souls at absolutely no cost to us, too. Knowing that we are prone to pay an unnecessarily enormous price for those things which we assume will satisfy only to find out that they have caught us in their traps while delivering nothing, He welcomes us to "come, buy wine and milk without money and without cost."

When Jesus appeared on the scene, the theme of feeding and nourishing our souls only intensified. In the story of how Jesus fed the multitudes with five loaves and two fish (John 6), we gather that Jesus openly and unabashedly acknowledges our hungers and proposes to satisfy them singlehandedly. Then, as He masterfully changed the subject from feeding grumbling bellies to feeding famished souls, He announced how the feeding would occur. Once again without any cost on our part, Jesus promised to feed us with a food that "endures to eternal life." And we would receive that eternal satisfaction by *eating Him.*

How do we eat Jesus? The skeptical crowd following after Jesus for more fish and chips to feed their grumbling tummies had the same question. Here is how Jesus responded to them:

Jesus said to them,
"I am the bread of life;
he who comes to Me shall not hunger,
and he who believes in Me shall never thirst."
(John 6:35)

The only way Jesus can ever satisfy our hungry souls is if we first *believe* He is who He says He is and that He can do all He says He can do. We must acknowledge that nothing else satisfies the way He can. We have to abandon all other means of satisfaction and trust fully that He indeed has what it takes to meet our needs…singlehandedly.

Then, according to the same passage, we have to cease going to all the other things we have been running after in order to have our hungry souls temporarily satisfied, and *go* to Him instead. Many of us claim Jesus can satisfy us, sing songs about Him satisfying us, quote verses from the Bible about how He meets our needs, and even encourage others to take their needs to Jesus, but we fail to *go to Him* with our hungry, parched, and needy souls. Sure, we run to Him with our financial woes, our health concerns, our relationship struggles, and our problems at work. We may ask Him to provide us with things like wisdom and direction and money. But do we run to Him and Him alone when we are aching for a little significance? Do we turn to Him when we feel lonely and unloved? Do we hold our empty cup out to Him when we simply need a little attention, a nod of approval, some TLC? Or do we do like God's chosen people had resorted to doing in Jeremiah 2? Do we walk after emptiness and in the process become empty (Jeremiah 2:5)? It is not enough to believe Jesus *can* satisfy our souls; we must *go to Him* so He can.

But once we do bend the knee, confess that He is quite capable of feeding our famished souls, and ask Him to do so, how do we actually eat Him? How do we feed on the Bread of Life?

How Do We Eat the Bread of Life?

We find the answer to that important question by responsibly and accurately stringing together a few carefully chosen and significant Scripture passages which all speak to this issue. Consider the implications when you add the following verses together much the way you would a mathematical equation.

"I {Jesus} am the bread of life."
(John 6:48)

+

"I {Jesus} am the living bread that came down out of heaven; if anyone eats of this bread, he shall live forever; and the bread also which I shall give for the life of the world is my flesh." (John 6:51)

+

In the beginning was the Word,
and the Word was with God,
and the Word was God. (John 1:1)

+

And the Word became flesh,
and dwelt among us,
and we beheld His glory,
glory as of the only begotten from the Father,
full of grace and truth. (John 1:14)

+

...man does not live by bread alone,
but man lives by everything
that proceeds out of the mouth of the Lord.
(Deuteronomy 8:3)

In order to live abundant and satisfied lives, we must learn to *eat* God's Word. Eating the Word of God requires more than just reading it. We must even do more than study it. In order to eat—chew on, swallow, and digest—God's Word, we must learn to *meditate* on it. Like David, the one who attested that God had so faithfully satisfied his soul, we must develop the skill of delighting in God's Word and thinking on it day and night so we become like well watered, flourishing trees planted by a steady, flowing stream of refreshing water. (See Psalm 1:2-3)

But before we talk about how to meditate on God's Word, there is one other condition for eating "the Word" which we must discuss. While our scripture equation strung together on previous pages is correct, it is incomplete. We must add one parenthetical condition to our equation. And if you'll remember from your days in math class, the work in the parentheses has to be done first!

+

(And my God shall supply all your needs according to His riches in glory in Christ Jesus.*)*
(Philippians 4:1; parentheses mine, added for effect)

Just memorizing and meditating on Scripture verses will not feed your hungry soul. Undoubtedly, many have tried to find satisfaction in the Bible only eventually to put it down in frustration. You see, the only way digesting the precepts and promises of Scripture will satisfy your soul is if you do so *within the context of a relationship with Jesus Christ.* Apart from that relationship, God is under no obligation to satisfy your soul through His Word. He wants to satisfy you completely, but will only do so if you have come to Him through His Son Jesus.

Jesus Himself said that He is the way to God and no one could come to God (for satisfaction, salvation, anything) except through Him (John 14:6). If you have yet to commit your life to Jesus as your Savior and Lord, please turn to page 151 in this book to find out how you can begin that crucial relationship. Trust me, God wants to satisfy your soul, and He can indeed do so singlehandedly. But you will find no satisfaction outside of a vital and growing relationship with

Jesus. On the other hand, once you begin a relationship with God through Jesus Christ, you can experience deep and abiding satisfaction every day.

How This Book Works

The purpose of this short devotional book is to help you develop the habit of meditating on God's Word so He can satisfy your hungry soul every day with His daily bread. It is my hope that by choosing to fill your soul with these scriptures each day for 31 consecutive days, you will become convinced that Jesus is indeed the One who can satisfy your hungers like no other.

But in order for Jesus to satisfy your soul through His Word, He asks that you forsake all other attempts to meet your souls' desires and allow Him to fill those hollow places on His own. He asks that you abandon the dry, cracked and empty cisterns you have dug with your own two hands in an attempt to find soul-quenching refreshment, and turn to Him, the Living Water, instead.

So before you begin this 31-day journey, I suggest you take a few minutes to go before the Lord and seek His guidance in abandoning your cracked and empty cisterns. Like David in Psalm 139:23-24, say to God,

Search me, O God, and know my heart;
Try me and know my anxious thoughts;
And see if there be any hurtful way in me,
And lead me in the everlasting way.

And if He points out to you any "hurtful way," any path you have blazed in an effort to seek soul satisfaction from something or someone else, confess that to Him and abandon it immediately. It will not be easy. Like the woman Jesus encountered at the well in John 4, you may have to come to terms with a string of unhealthy relationships from which you have sought a little love, affirmation or intimacy. Or, like the writer of Ecclesiastes, you may have to admit you have sought purpose and significance from money, work, possessions, or accomplishment. Or, like the people of Israel and Judah, God may convict you of any number of other idols you have formed and bowed down to in order to gain a little security, an ounce of peace, or a feeling of hope, false and fleeting as it may have been. Whatever God brings to your attention as an empty and unfulfilling source of satisfaction, allow Him to loosen your grip on it and relinquish it to Him.

Then, with your back to the broken and empty cisterns of your past, turn to Jesus. *Believe* He can satisfy your soul and *go to Him alone* for satisfaction. Meet Him in the pages of His Word and trust that He is speaking soul-satisfying truth to you there. Drink in what He says to you, allowing it to settle deep into the parched places of your soul. Experience the refreshment, savor it, and drink in some more. Then enjoy the effervescent effects of it overflowing from your life into the lives of others around you. The abundant and overflowing life—that is what true satisfaction is all about.

The Ins and Outs of Scripture Meditation

For the next 31 days I will supply you with a soul-satisfying passage of Scripture. It is crucial that you read and meditate on those verses. But I have also written my interpretation of that daily bread for you to read. You will find that each devotional entry is written as though Jesus is speaking directly to you.

I have written in this format because I have found it to work tremendously in my own life. I have read several other devotional books written as messages directly from God, including Sarah Young's *Jesus Calling*, and I have found they help me hear His message to me fresh and anew. I do not suppose that my words are on an equal plane as His, nor do I want you to read my words as though they are inerrant and exhaustive commentary on His infallible and Holy Word. I simply write in the first person from Jesus' perspective so you can feel the intimacy expressed in His Holy Word in a fresh context. In these devotional writings, "I", "Me", "My", and "Myself", refer to Jesus and "you" refers to you the reader.

Meditate on His words. Think of chewing on them, swallowing them, and digesting them.

Here is how I picture the process:

1. **Put your napkin in your lap.** Prepare to hear from the Lord by asking the Holy Spirit to speak to you. Give Him permission to reach deep into your soul and speak to you in the inner person. Anticipate a fresh word from the Lord.

2. **Take a bite.** Read the focal Scripture passage carefully, slowly, with anticipation and hunger.

3. **Chew on it.** Begin to meditate on the chosen passage by reading my words if you wish. Or you may not need to read what I have written right away. God can surely speak directly to you through His Word as well as He can to me. But one way or the other, take the time to ask the simple question, "What is He saying to me?" Read the passage as if you are reading a letter from someone who loves you dearly.

4. **Swallow it.** We swallow God's Word when we accept it as truth. After you have read the selected passage and my interpretation of His message to you, decide if you believe what God is saying—and I hope you do. However, even if you find God's message hard to

fathom, circumstances say otherwise, other people cast doubts, or you just *feel* His Word cannot possibly be true, choose to believe that God is who He says He is and that He can do what He says He will do…even in your situation. Swallow it! As you "swallow" the passage, I encourage you to write a brief explanation or prayer about *how* you are swallowing it. What are you choosing to believe? How is this particular truth feeding your soul?

5. **Digest it.** Try to return to the scripture throughout your day. David said he meditated on God's Word morning and night. I suggest you buy a set of 4x6 index cards before you get started and write at least part of each day's Scripture passage on a card as you go through the book. Put those cards into a small photo album and carry it with you through the day so you can refer to these tasty morsels as you go about your day's activities. Digestion does not happen immediately; it takes time.

6. **Fortify that first bite with a few more.** Beyond the focal scripture passage, I have provided other supplemental passages that reinforce the truths presented in the first. I suggest you read these in your Bible, reflecting on them as well. You also might find scriptures here that you want to write on a 4x6 index card and add to your album. It is important that you feast upon the entire breadth of God's Word, so I have tried to supply you with scriptures from both the Old and New Testaments each day.

7. **Pour forth.** While I love a good, tasty meal, I realize we do not eat just for the fun of it. We eat in order to

> have energy so we can then expend that energy in fruitful activity. In the same way, when we nourish our souls to the point of overflowing satisfaction, we need to turn that nourishment into energetic activity for the Lord. As you feast on God's Word, you will find that your soul is so satisfied you cannot help but spill out what you have gained. Like a "spring of water whose waters do not fail" (Isaiah 58:11), you will have plenty of love, energy, selflessness, zeal, and joy to serve others, share from your resources, and glorify God in all you do. I suggest you even share each day's chosen Scripture passage with someone you encounter during your day. When you speak it and explain it to someone else, you will find yourself drawing even more satisfaction from it.

I hope you will learn how to meditate on God's Word in such a way that you develop a lifetime habit of feasting on His soul-satisfying truth. In order to develop that habit, I will share some closing thoughts with you at the end of these 31 days on how to continue to feed yourself a steady diet of the Bread of Life. Meanwhile, let me encourage you to get those 4x6 index cards and a small photo album so you can begin building a menu of soul-satisfying Scripture from which you can continue to dine.

It is my prayer that at the end of these 31 days you will be able to say along with Jeremiah,

Thy words were found and I ate them,
And Thy words became for me a joy
and the delight of my heart...
(Jeremiah 15:16a)

When you long
for unconditional,
extravagant,
and passionate
love...

"God is love..."
1 John 4:16

Day 1

The Lord appeared to him from afar, saying, "I have loved you with an everlasting love; therefore I have drawn you with lovingkindness." (Jeremiah 31:3)

I am wild about you! My love for you is bigger than you can possibly fathom. You can never exhaust the depths of my love for you nor move beyond the borders of its reach. I love you with a mighty big love.

While I know you may greatly desire for others to love you with such a huge love, it will never happen. Only I have the capacity to love you so completely, so unselfishly, so consistently. Out of My love for you I have carefully and intentionally placed people in your life who love you with a good and warm love. Depending on My carefully and lovingly devised plans for your life, I may have blessed you with a spouse, children, parents, grandchildren, siblings, or good friends who love you well. But none of these people will ever love you the way I do. They will fail you, disappoint you, behave selfishly at times, leave you some day, or even just neglect to give you all the attention and affection you desire. Try as they may, they cannot love you with the perfect, unconditional love I offer. My love never fails.

I have not placed these people in your life to put them in competition with Myself. There is no need for comparison and rivalry. Please do not let such an atmosphere of competition develop. You control that. If you will love Me with all your heart, soul, and mind, you will find you are also free to enjoy the relationships with people I have given you. But if you seek from them a love greater than they can give, both you and they will grow frustrated and eventually bitter. Instead, come to Me for so great a love.

Especially as a woman, you desire to be wooed and courted. If you think back through the days of your life, you will see evidence of how I have drawn you to Myself with lovingkindness. I have gone out of My way to do the subtle and little things, the extravagant and splashy things, the unique things, and the deeply significant things necessary to draw you personally to Me. I have done all of those things because you are worth pursuing. I love you.

I want you to realize just how personal My love for you is. You will begin to grasp the personal nature of My affection for you when you begin to notice all the concrete things My love gives you. Because I love you with an everlasting and pursuing love, you can be assured that I think of you constantly; I guard you and hold you dear like the apple of My eye; I make good plans for you and see to it that those plans are carried through without deviation; and I provide for your every need out of My abundant riches.

Despite the hype from romantic movies, romance novels, or fairytales, there is no greater love than the love I have for you. I have chosen to love you despite all your faults. And I do not insist you clean up before I will shower you with kindness and affection. My love is unconditional. I do not hold a little back, promising to love you more when you get your act together. My love truly surpasses your greatest expectations. And if you are worried about how I could possibly love you with that big of a love and still love others just as much, don't. Just rest in the fact that I do love you—the individual you are. I love you.

Questions to ponder:
Looking back, how do you notice God pursuing you?

What has He done recently to express His love to you?

Additional scriptures to feast upon today:

1 Corinthians 13:8, 13
Romans 8:38-39
Psalm 17:8
Zechariah 2:8

As I swallow these scriptures, I am believing...

Day 2

"Greater love has no one than this, that one lay down his life for his friends." (John 15:13)

Most people find it flattering to hear someone say they love them enough to die for them. But, of course, you would hope that the person would never have to prove that love with such a costly sacrifice. Because you love that person in turn, you would not want them to die. But I did not ask if you would want Me to die for you because I knew you would never understand just how necessary it was. I just did it. I died for you.

Why did I die for you? Was it just because the Father told Me to? Was it only because there had to be some atonement for your sins, some sufficient sacrifice to pay the penalty you had acquired? Yes, both of those reasons were enough to lead Me to the cross. But the greater reason for which I died for you is simply that I wanted to restore the relationship you had broken with Me and My Father through your sin. I wanted, out of a huge and compelling love, for the fellowship between you and Me, the Father, and the Holy Spirit to be restored. That relationship is important to Me. You are important to Me.

That is why I now call you "friend." My death on the cross renews the friendship that had been lost due to your sin. If I had not died on the cross, as much as I love you, we would still forever be at odds. We would not be friends. We would not be a family. But because I love you and because I love My Father, I wanted to restore that relationship. No, I did not have to leave the comfort of heaven for you, but I did. I certainly did not have to bear the reproach of your sin, but I did. And I loathed feeling the Father's scorn as I bore that sin, but the discomfort did not keep Me from bearing your sin all the same. I love you that much.

Usually if someone dies for another, it is to prevent that person from having to die. For instance, someone would say he would take a bullet for her, jump in front of a train and push her out of the way, or take the beating while she ran. But I did not just die for you so that you would not die. Truthfully, you may die one day…at least in earthly, physical terms. But I died so you can *live*…abundantly…forever…in a sweet, satisfying and perfectly restored relationship with God. I did not die just to *spare* you from pain of some sort. I died to *give* you something good and sweet and lovely.

And in case there is any question in your mind, that sacrifice was completely worth it for Me. I have no regrets. I still look upon you every day as my precious, redeemed bride. I long to return for you, to bring you home to heaven with Me, to unite with you like never before. And even when you do things you regret, say things you shouldn't, forget about Me, or chase after empty and vain things, I love you no less. I yearn for you to return to Me with a passionate and reciprocal love, but I do not for one minute regret the price I paid for you. I am your Redeemer and you are My beloved. And you are worth the price I paid. I love you.

Questions to ponder:
How does it make you feel to know Jesus died for you so you could have a relationship with Him?

Additional scriptures to feast upon today:

John 3:16
John 15:13-16
Romans 5:8
1 John 4:7-16

As I swallow these scriptures, I am believing…

Day 3

But Thou, O Lord, art a God merciful and gracious, slow to anger and abundant in lovingkindness and truth. (Psalm 86:15)

Today, as you go through your day, keep in mind that I am quite mindful of your frame. I created you, so I know you are made of dust. You are human, not perfect, and prone to wander, prone to stray. And when you do, you can rest assured that I will be quick and generous to offer you forgiveness, extend grace, and show mercy.

By nature I am gracious and merciful. On a good day you might manage to forgive someone you love if you humble yourself and lay down your rights. But I do not have to muster up mercy. I simply *am* merciful. I extend mercy freely, without strings, without reproach. I give it graciously—as much as you can ever need and more. I keep no record of your wrongs, but separate your mistakes from you as far as the east is from the west. Try as you might to persuade Me to do otherwise, I will not recall your offenses and bring them up against you again. I ask you not to bring them up again either. Trust Me, the price I paid for your sins was sufficient. There need be no other sacrifice, penance, or punishment.

Because I am gracious by nature, My mercy might appear to be cheap…at first glance. But when you consider that I am a holy and blameless God who has loved you without fail, you will become aware of just how much forgiveness costs Me. Your sins do not just hurt My feelings, but instead they offend Me greatly. They fly in the face of My holiness, My righteousness, My pure and passionate love for you. And they cost Me My life, shame on the cross, and separation from My Father. I won't make light of it. My death on the cross was no small price to pay. So when I show you mercy and grace, you can know it is out of a heart abounding with love. Because I love you, I show you mercy.

I know that at times you seek mercy and forgiveness from the people in your life, only to find it given grudgingly, if at all. Hang in there. Even if people cannot quite forgive you, I can. Do not allow their inability to forgive and move on to convince you that I also have not forgiven you. That is a deception of the enemy meant to keep you bogged down in the mire of guilt. That is not My desire for you.

My forgiveness of your sins is an act of love. Please relish that forgiveness. Lift your head; do not hang it in shame. My mercy is an invitation to you to join the dance again. Take My hand, let Me wrap My arms around you and twirl you around the dance floor with joyful abandonment. I love you so I have showered you with grace and mercy! Won't you dance with Me today?

Questions to ponder:
How has God shown you mercy recently?

What gracious things has He done on your behalf? What has He generously given you that you do not deserve?

Additional scriptures to feast upon today:

Ephesians 2:4-7
Psalm 51:12
Psalm 86:15
Psalm 103:1-14

As I swallow these scriptures, I am believing...

Day 4

The Spirit Himself bears witness with our spirit that we are children of God. (Romans 8:16)

I created you in *Our* image—the image of the Father, the Son, and the Holy Spirit. That is why one of your most basic needs is to be part of a family. Just like the Father, the Son and the Holy Spirit are one; you crave to be one with another, with others. I put that hunger in you and it is a hunger I want to satisfy.

I may have given you parents, siblings, and extended family members with whom you share a history. You may have been blessed with a spouse, children and even grandchildren with whom you have made a home. These relationships are all blessings that I bestow as I see fit. But, undoubtedly, even those family members whom you love have disappointed you at times. Perhaps they have withdrawn, moved away, or simply grown apart from you. Maybe some of them have even neglected you, hurt you, abandoned you, or severed their relationship with you. And in time, you will lose their earthly presence…if you have not already.

But I have brought you into My family with love and open arms. I have chosen you, adopted you. You are no step child. I have bestowed upon you the full rights and privileges of family. You are My child and you may call Me Abba, Daddy. I want you to feel that close to Me.

I want you to come to Me when things are broken and trust Me to fix them, even make them brand new. I want you to snuggle close to Me for affection. I want you to cry out to Me when you are scared. And I want you to run to Me with your aching heart when someone calls you names, leaves you out, or hurts your feelings in any way.

I look out for your best interest at all times. You are My priority. I will help you grow, thrive, and succeed. I will always be here for you; I will never abandon you. I am forever in your corner.

And unlike your earthly parents who have their human faults and make mistakes along the way, I will never be late, never forget you, always have the answers, always have time for you, and always meet your every need. I have obligated Myself to do those things for you, but I also do them willingly because I love you, My child.

As My child you are invited to take a seat at My table. I want to feed your soul with good things, delicious things. You are not to see yourself as one of the household servants, but you are to sit at My table as My child.

And My care for you does not end here. I am preparing great and wonderful things for you. You are a rightful heir of all I have to bestow. I am preparing a place for you in heaven so you can live eternally in the shelter of My home and as part of My family.

Will you let Me feed your desire for family love? Will you look to Me as your Father, your Daddy? Will you hold tight to My hand today, knowing you have a Father who adores you, who has your back, and who longs to shelter you from the storms? I love you.

Questions to ponder:
How has God shown Himself to be a loving Father to you recently?

Additional scriptures to feast upon today:

Genesis 1:26-31
Romans 8:14-17
1 John 3:1-2

As I swallow these scriptures, I am believing…

Day 5

The Lord your God is in your midst, a victorious warrior. He will exult over you with joy, He will be quiet in His love, He will rejoice over you with shouts of joy.
(Zephaniah 3:17)

Are you looking for your knight in shining armor? One who can ride in to sweep you off your feet and rescue you from impending harm? One who will fight your foes and defend your dignity? One who will treat you like a lady and hold your villains in contempt?

Look no further.

Believe it or not, I have already fought hard for you. I have already rescued you from your greatest foe's power and imprisonment. I have set you free from his reach and, if only you will call out to Me in your moments of distress, I will not allow him to have any more power over you. You need not be anxious or feel threatened any more. My perfect love for you has cast aside any need for fear. And because I have fought the ultimate battle over life's final foe, you are free to live without the shackles of death. You may dance and love and give and laugh and sing, all because I have overcome all that once held you prisoner.

But in this life, until I ride in on My white charger to take you home with Me to live in Paradise forevermore, you will have trials. Life will surely have its ups and downs. There may even be days when you feel as if you are certainly under attack, as if the whole world is against you. The prince of this world continues to rule his mock kingdom and to bully his way around, trying to impose fear and dread upon those I love and call My own. He will try to convince you that you are without hope, without a future, without recourse. Do not listen to his deceptions.

Instead, call upon Me. I have paid a large price for you and called you by name. You are Mine and I take full responsibility in your battles. When life's circumstances seem to plunge you into a raging river, I will be with you. When you feel as if you are walking through a fiery storm, I will protect you and not allow you to be scorched, much less destroyed.

Why will I always and consistently come to your aid? Because I love you and you are so very precious to Me. I will go to great lengths to honor you, to treat you like a lady, to show everyone around you that I love you. You are so loved.

But not only will I fight for you; I will also strengthen you in the inner woman so you can stand strong, with dignity and valor, in the face of daunting circumstances. When the earth around you seems to shake with tragedy, sorrow, and trouble, My love will keep you firmly rooted. And then, in your darkest and most volatile circumstances, you will catch a glimpse of just how broad and long and high and deep My love is for you. Oh, that you would grasp how much I adore you! Then you would be filled up with all the fullness I have to offer.

Let Me be your strong and devoted warrior king. Truly, I am able to exceed even your greatest desires for heroism. Won't you rest in My deep and abiding and abundant love for you today?

Questions to ponder:
Have you seen Jesus as your knight in shining armor? How has He fought for you in the past?

What battle do you need for Him to fight for you today?

Additional scriptures to feast upon today:

Isaiah 43:1-4a
Ephesians 3:14-21

As I swallow these scriptures, I am believing...

Day 6

Behold, I have inscribed you on the palms of My hands;
Your walls are continually before Me.
(Isaiah 49:16)

Oh, to be known, truly known through and through, and to know another in the same way! You were created for such intimacy. My Father and the Holy Spirit and I are One. We are distinct and individual, and yet We are intertwined in intimacy. And so it is Our design that you also experience intimacy with Us.

As My Father and I are one, We desire for you to be one with Us also. We invite you to abide with Us, to stay close and draw from Us. And in that kind of intimacy you will not just survive, but you will thrive. You will have a fruitful, meaningful, and passionate life. Do you want that kind of life? Dwelling with Us, *in* Us is where you will find it.

You can feel safe with Me. You can draw close, bare all, be yourself, let down your guard, and breathe a sigh of relief in My presence. All things are laid bare before Me anyhow. And you can find comfort in knowing that I am not one to mock you in your weaknesses or sigh with disappointment at your failures. I have been there. I have walked with human feet on the same sod you trod, so I know how difficult life can be, how temptations can pull at you, how friends can disappoint and hurt you, how life can get scary and uncertain. And while I walked that path without ever once giving in to temptation, I have compassion for you when you do. After all, I know your frame, that you are but human. I created you. And I love you.

Not only do I invite you to be intimately transparent with Me, but I offer to be equally forthright with you. Through My Spirit who indwells you, I give you insight into My heart, My mind, My ways. I am freely giving you My thoughts, which can only be understood by those who have My Spirit to disclose such things to them. Have you ever been jealous of someone who seems to have wonderful, magical secrets with another? Put such jealousies away, My love! You have just such an intimate relationship with Me…if you so choose.

Do you ever feel forgotten, overlooked? Do you ever feel lonely, not so much on a physical level, but on a more intimate level? Like no one else completely "gets you" or evens hears you correctly? Well I want you to know that I love you with such a compelling love that I could never forget you. Who you are—through and through—is inscribed on the palms of My hands. You are always on My mind, in My thoughts. And I do get you. I know what makes you happy, nervous, angry, sad, and uncertain. I know the things you worry about, the dreams you have, the disappointments you have faced, the memories you treasure in your heart, the hopes you continue to fan, and the losses you try not to count. I know. I know. And I want you to find comfort in My intimate knowledge of you coupled with My tender love for you. That, precious one, is what true, safe, and loving intimacy is all about. And you will only find it in Me.

Questions to ponder:
How does it make you feel to consider Jesus' intimate knowledge of you coupled with His tender love for you?

Do you have a secret you need to share with Him today? Do you have something you need to tell someone safe so you can breathe a little more easily? Will you tell Him now?

Additional scriptures to feast upon today:

Psalm 56:8
Psalm 73:28
John 15:9-11
John 17:20-21
Hebrews 4:13-16

As I swallow these scriptures, I am believing…

When your world feels unsettled and you need something or someone to hold onto for security...

"The name of the Lord is a strong tower;
The righteous runs into it and is safe."
Proverbs 18:10

Day 7

Bless the Lord, O my soul!
O Lord my God, Thou art very great;
Thou art clothed with splendor and majesty.
(Psalm 104:1)

You have a very big God. You need to grasp that. I have stretched out the heavens like a tent and established the earth securely upon its foundations. I covered the earth with deep waters, but then rebuked those very waters until they fled to their boundaries. With but a word I brought forth mountains and laid out valleys, sending streams to flow between them to give drink to every animal of the field. I ordered your days into seasons for planting, growing, harvesting, and resting. I have created, sustained, renewed, and even killed. I hold the world in My hands. The earth is Mine and all that is in it. I am a mighty and big God.

I am God and you are not. Do not be offended by that truth. Instead, rest in that knowledge. Relax. Not only do you not have to hold *the* world together, but you do not even have to hold *your* world together. Just as I sustain the world around you by causing the sun to rise and set each day, I will hold your life in the palm of My capable hand. I alone am able to restrain evil men from hurting you, to reprove those who cause you pain, to issue boundaries to those who would impose upon you, and to build walls of safety around you when evil creeps in close. I am able and I am more than willing.

I am sovereign. Do you really understand what that means? It does not mean that I dangle you from marionette strings and laugh as you obligingly do My will. It simply means that I am ultimately in charge and nothing happens to you, My beloved, without My loving consent. Everything that comes into your life—both good and bad, joyful and sad—comes sifted through My fingers in love. And everything I allow into your life is only permitted if it will help Me accomplish My good and perfect will, which is ultimately to make you more like Myself.

Quite frankly, many are offended by My power and might, My sovereignty, and My greatness. But I ask you, oh child whom I love, to embrace those things instead. Let My strength be a rock of refuge, My sovereignty a life buoy to cling to when things seem out of control, and My greatness a beacon in an ever-dimming world. With Me in control, you can relax, breathe, and quit looking over your shoulder. And then you can really live.

So loosen your grip and hand the controls over to Me. You can trust Me. I am a mighty and big God. And I have your back.

Questions to ponder:
What impresses you the most about God? What makes Him big in your eyes?

How do you need to loosen your grip on the controls of your life today?

Additional scriptures to feast upon today:

Psalm 71:19
Psalm 73:25-28
Psalm 105:14-15
Psalm 115:11-13

As I swallow these scriptures, I am believing…

Day 8

God is our refuge and strength,
A very present help in trouble.
(Psalm 46:1)

Does the ground you walk on sometimes seem a little shaky? Whether you are uncertain about what the future holds, uncomfortable with today's circumstances, or still fretting over past problems, it is easy to feel the reverberations of this ever-shifting world. Nothing stays the same. No one is completely reliable. No day holds exactly the same itinerary as the day before. It is no wonder you reach out for something to grab hold of, something sure and grounded.

Reach for Me. Grab hold of Me. I am your rock, your fortress, your source of strength and stability.

I know you are wondering how you can reach out for a God you cannot see or physically touch. I will tell you how. As I have said in My Word, My name is a strong tower and you need to run to it for safety. Do you know My name? Do you know (that you know that you know that you know) that My name is El Shaddai, the all-sufficient One? Do you know that name deep in your soul so you do not worry and fret, but instead you run to Me, your all-sufficient, perfect, completely capable and able God, El Shaddai?

I am also Jehovah Jireh, the God who provides…always… completely…perfectly. I am Jehovah Rapha, the God who heals… every disease…eventually…wholly. I am El Roi, the God who sees… everything…even into the hearts of men…even in the dark places…even when you cannot see. And I am Jehovah Shalom, the God of peace…in the midst of conflict…in the middle of the storm …when you are anxious and worried and can find no peace.

So here is what you need to know: the better you know Me, the easier it will be for you to climb the stairs of My strong fortress to find asylum, peace, refuge, and perspective. Sure, there is power in My name. And if you just want to call out My name, I will certainly heed your cry and come to your aid. But you will find so much more security in running to Me once you know exactly whom you are running toward.

Spend time with Me, My child. Get to know Me. I want to make Myself known to you. Spend time in My Word. Read the accounts in the Old Testament of how I revealed Myself to My people, Israel. Read the gospel accounts of when I walked the roads of Galilee and interacted with the disciples, the religious leaders, the hurting and hungry, the children, and the skeptics. Meet Me in the pages of My Word, from Genesis to Revelation, and I will show you just who I am.

And as you come to know Me more and more each day, reach out to Me. Run to Me. I will be the one thing you can count on, the strong and mighty fortress, though the earth should change and the mountains should slip into the heart of the seas, though the waters might roar and foam and the mountains should quake and shift. I will always be your Rock.

Questions to ponder:
Which of the names of God presented in this devotional means the most to you today? Why?

How does knowing who God is help you be able to run to Him like a strong fortress?

Additional scriptures to feast upon today:

Psalm 46:1-3
Psalm 55:22
Psalm 61:1-4
Proverbs 18:10

As I swallow these scriptures, I am believing...

Day 9

And you have seen all that the Lord your God has done to all these nations because of you, for the Lord your God is He who has been fighting for you. (Joshua 23:3)

I am *for* you. I hope such faithfulness encourages and strengthens you. I know there must be days when it seems that everyone is against you or at least that no one is truly, one hundred percent for you. But I am.

Truly, you must fight your share of battles in this world. Keep in mind that the enemy is not flesh and blood—your disconnected husband, your demanding boss, your disobedient child, your dramatic sister, or your disagreeable co-worker—but the spiritual powers of this world. The devil is out to steal, kill and destroy—your joy, your testimony, your marriage, your family, your church…anything I have established—and you must stand firm against him. You will have to wage these very real battles with spiritual weapons, which find their basis in My Word and prayer.

Still, there may be times when people lend themselves to the schemes of the enemy, and their words, actions, and attitudes hurt you like the sharp edge of a sword. In those times, you may feel the urge to pick up your worldly weapons—piercing glares, cutting dismissals, jabbing sarcasm, poisonous slander, razor sharp accusations, biting remarks—and fight back. Don't.

These are battles you must let Me fight for you. I promise to defend your honor, preserve your integrity, protect your heart, and shield you from any fatal blows. But you must not stoop to rolling around in the dirt with other people, regardless of how enemy-like they may seem. I repeat: they are *not* the real enemy.

In fact, they are people I love. Sometimes that may be hard for you to fathom, considering they have treated you rather poorly. In fact, they may have done you great harm, serious injury. Still I love them. And, to the extent they will let Me, I am at work in their lives, drawing them to Me, teaching them about My love, giving mercy, offering them salvation, and creating in them a new heart. And, to put it to you gently, when you pull out your weapons and start fighting back, your interference hinders My work in their lives. So I am asking you to refrain from fighting against the flesh and blood "enemies," even though they may call you out.

The only way you are going to be able to do what I am asking here is if you truly believe with your heart of hearts that *I* will fight for you. You must remember that I have paid the ultimate price for you. You are My prized possession. I have sought you and redeemed you. I am not about to let anyone destroy what I have bought at so high a price.

Not only that, but I *want* to fight for you. I want to help you gain new ground, conquer lingering foes, and establish your presence in your promised land. Remember, I am *for* you.

Questions to ponder:
Have you seen God fight a battle for you? How did you know He was fighting for you?

Is there a battle going on now which you need Him to fight for you? Have you asked Him to step in?

Additional scriptures to feast upon today:

Exodus 14:14
Deuteronomy 3:22
Psalm 118:5-9
Isaiah 30:15
Romans 8:28

As I swallow these scriptures, I am believing…

Day 10

Behold, God is my helper;
The Lord is the sustainer of my soul.
(Psalm 54:4)

Cast your burden upon Me. I am strong and able to sustain you through every overwhelming and difficult situation. In fact, I will be your strength. I will infuse you with supernatural stamina so you may victoriously walk through any storm you encounter.

It is understandable that you may sometimes feel heavy-hearted, weary, spent, and overwhelmed. Life is hard in this broken world. But I do not leave you to fend for yourself. I am only a sigh for relief away. Simply cast and release. Cast your burden upon Me and leave it with Me. Allow Me to carry it for you. Do not just tell Me about it; give it to Me. Give it all to Me. If you do, I will never allow you to be shaken. I will hold both the burden and you in My big hands.

Sometimes you have more than one concern. Like a pair of rabbits in a cage, your anxieties multiply in your mind as you mull them over, try to diagnose them, struggle to solve them, and ponder their long-term effects. You do not have to suffer such angst, you know. Allow Me to console you in your distress, and you will once again delight in life. Can you imagine finding delight in the midst of your struggles? If you will willingly and completely hand your problems over to Me, I guarantee that you can once again smile, laugh, dance, sing.

Admittedly, there are times when even I put a lot on your plate. I require much from you in order to stretch you, grow you, and use you in powerful ways. I want to display My strength through you so others can see and be drawn to Me. If I give you much to handle, many things to accomplish, or much to survive, you can rest assured that I will also graciously give you everything you need for those assignments. In fact, I will give you an abundance of whatever the ordeal may call for—strength, stamina, knowledge, wisdom, patience, compassion, forbearance, love, you name it—so you even have enough to share with those around you. The result? My grace made sufficient in you will result in a harvest of good things all around you. You and those you influence will be rolling in My riches. You will get to see My glory. And you will know Me more intimately than ever before.

So walk with Me today. Allow Me to walk alongside you. I will give you work to do, but it will seem easy as long as we are together. Meanwhile, I will shoulder your burdens, for My shoulders are broad and strong. And as we walk together, you will find rest for your soul. That is what I offer you today—rest for your weary soul.

Questions to ponder:

What burdens are weighing you down today? Have you given them to Him?

To what difficult task has He called you during this season of life? How has He graciously given you what you need to accomplish it?

Additional scriptures to feast upon today:

Psalm 55:4-8, 22
Psalm 94:19
Isaiah 41:10
Matthew 11:28-30
2 Corinthians 9:8

As I swallow these scriptures, I am believing...

Day 11

How great is Thy goodness,
Which Thou hast stored up for those who fear Thee,
Which Thou hast wrought for those who take refuge in Thee,
Before the sons of men!
(Psalm 31:19)

I know no other way to put it, but to say, "I am good." And I long to be good to you. I want to fill your days with good things, to shower you with goodness, and to be good to your soul.

I want you to find stability in My goodness. I am aware that people sometimes behave well and sometimes do not. You are no different, of course. But even when others are treating you poorly, you can *rest* in My goodness. You do not have to worry about how I will behave on any given day or how I will respond to you. I am consistently good.

Take courage and face your day with My goodness as your anchor. Face the fickleness of others with forbearance. Stare down the evil in the world with victory. And courageously venture into your mission field because you do not *have* to be treated well by anyone else. I will be good to you even when you can find no other source of good in this world. Even when everything and everyone else seems to be tainted by the evil of the powers of this present age, you can count on My goodness. Does that assurance give you comfort? I hope so. And here is an added benefit. Wherever you do venture, My goodness and mercy will follow you. I am right on you with all the good that

I am, so where you go, My goodness goes, too. Because of Me in you, you can do some good in this world.

I am working good *in* you, too. I can take all the bad, all the good, all the surprising, and all the confusing things that come your way and work with those things to produce that which is one hundred percent, through and through, beautifully and uniquely good for you. I can make everything turn out for your benefit. Now, I will admit there will be times when you will not see the good at first, but you can trust Me. Why? Because I am good…all the time. And all the time…I am good.

I also wish to bless you with good and lovely gifts. I will do you good all the days of your life. In other words, it doesn't have to rain for Me to send you a rainbow. I will remind you of My faithfulness and goodness toward you every day…if you will only look persistently for those displays of My affection. Are you looking? And you do not have to be good in order for Me to be good. Oh, I smile when you do good and display My goodness in your actions and words and attitudes. But if you are not good, I am still good. You can count on it.

Questions to ponder:
How have you witnessed God's goodness recently?

Why do you feel secure knowing that God is always, consistently, and thoroughly good?

Additional scriptures to feast upon today:

Exodus 33:19
Psalm 23:6
Matthew 7:11
John 10:11
James 1:17

As I swallow these scriptures, I am believing...

Day 12

Now to Him who is able to do exceeding abundantly beyond all that we ask or think, according to the power that works within us…
(Ephesians 3:20)

I never stop. I am always at work. And while I am indeed working throughout the world and in the lives of millions and millions of people, I am also industriously working in your world and in your life.

I am at work within you. I am in the process of softening your heart so that it is malleable, easy to penetrate and more prone to love. I am renewing your mind, weaning you off the things of this world and setting your mind on the things above, the things of real consequence. I am developing your gifts, strengthening your resolve, reproducing My character in you, and fine tuning your perspective.

Some days you yield to the chisel and sand paper of My work with sweet submission; other days you wrestle against Me. Still, I continue to work. I will never give up on you, never abandon the work I have started. You can count on Me completing the good work I have begun in you. I hope that promise comforts you, to know there is someone who never stops working on your behalf.

I am also at work *around* you. I am working in the lives of your family members, your friends, your brothers and sisters in Christ, your co-workers. And guess what? I am using you to help Me with that work. That is why it is so important for you to be aware of My work. I want you to participate with Me in the work I am doing in others' lives. How do you do that? By praying, submitting to My leadership, walking in My Spirit, speaking only truth, loving, forgiving, exercising your spiritual gifts, and simply saying "yes" to Me. I invite you to join Me in the most important work in the world: the work of saving and changing lives. Will you join Me?

Sometimes I am sure you want to see more evidence of My work than I am ready to reveal to you. You become impatient for Me to work according to your blueprints, on your timetable, and toward your specified results. But I ask you to trust Me instead. I guarantee you I am working even if you cannot yet see the finished product. Hold onto this promise: I am always at work doing abundantly beyond anything you have asked for or could ever even imagine. My plans are not the same as your plans and My ways are not your ways. Simply put, Mine are so much better, making your plans look unambitious and weak. Trust Me here. I do have plans for you and I know what I am doing. My plans are for you to prosper, to succeed. And I will finish what I have started.

So when the waiting is stressful and you are prone to cry out, "Will someone *do* something?" trust Me. I am always working.

Questions to ponder:
How do you feel more secure knowing that God is always at work on your behalf?

Is there a "project" you need to be assured that God is working on today? Have you told Him? You might also ask Him how you can best cooperate with His work there.

Additional scriptures to feast upon today:

Deuteronomy 32:4
Job 5:9
Psalm 121:1-4
Jeremiah 29:11
Philippians 1:6

As I swallow these scriptures, I am believing…

When you feel small and unnoticed and you long to feel significant and noteworthy ...

"{you are} honored in the sight of the Lord."
Isaiah 49:5

Day 13

Now then, if you will indeed obey My voice and keep My covenant, then you shall be My own possession among all the peoples, for all the earth is Mine.
(Exodus 19:5)

Indeed, I have created you unique, special, and divinely significant. But quite honestly, it is not so much *who* you are that gives you an honorable place in this world as it is *whose* you are. And you are Mine.

Do not be taken aback by that assertion. It is a good thing to belong to the God who created, sustains, and rules this world. I have sought you, drawn you to Myself, paid your ransom with a mind-boggling price, gifted you for a purpose, and am even now preparing for you an eternal home so you may live in My physical kingdom forever.

You are My own possession among all the peoples of the earth. While others are searching for somewhere to belong, someone to affirm them, someone to notice them, you have those things in Me. Metaphorically speaking, I will do more than leave the light on for you; I'll wait up for you. You do not have to ask me to sit in the bleachers and root you on; I'm already there and I'm your biggest fan. And you do not have to tug on my sleeve and beg for My undivided attention; My eye is attentively on you always—not like a mother who watches her child on the playground out of the side of her eye while carrying on a conversation with someone else, but with My full and undivided gaze.

You are My child and I am your Father. I have chosen you, adopted you, blessed you with all that is Mine, and called you with a purpose. I have redeemed you, washed away all that made you unclean, and lavished upon you the riches of My grace. And mind you, I own the cattle on a thousand hills…and so much more. The world is Mine and all that is in it. And I hold all that out to you.

Sweet child, are you struggling to belong in some crowd, among a certain group of people? Are you compromising your standards, pretending to be something you really are not or putting on a show just to win the approval of others? You do not need to do that. I, the God of this universe, call you Mine. You belong with Me.

Questions to ponder:
How important is it to you to belong? Why do you feel more important when you have a sense of belonging?

How do you feel more significant knowing that you belong to the God of this universe?

Additional scriptures to feast upon today:

Exodus 19:5-6
Isaiah 43:1
Ephesians 1:3-8
Philippians 3:20
Revelation 1:6

As I swallow these scriptures, I am believing…

Day 14

"Before I formed you in the womb I knew you,
And before you were born I consecrated you;
I have appointed you a prophet to the nations."
(Jeremiah 1:5)

You are My beloved creation. I have taken My time with you, forming you with intricate complexity. Like a favored painting in the eye of its artist, you are crafted with love, tenderness, passion, purpose, and joy.

I love who you are. Do not think for a moment that I do not know your frailties and the weaknesses in your structure. But I am not discouraged by them as others may appear to be. You are still a masterwork in My hands; while I have gladly given you purpose and meaning now, I still am at work on you, too. And every day, as you yield to My process, you are becoming more and more reflective of My glory. In other words, you are looking more and more like Me.

Rest assured I have made no mistakes in you. I do not make mistakes. You are perfectly created. Yes, it is true that sin has entered this world and you bear its marks. You do miss the target of godliness, holiness, at times. But I do not see you that way. Because you have been washed in the blood of your Savior, I see you as perfectly clean, beautiful, whole, and without blemish.

You are a Masterpiece and one day you will see yourself that way too. Until then, until I have removed the evil one and he has ceased to whisper his demeaning lies in your ears, I ask you to cling to these truths with a tight grip. You see, when you remember that you are a Masterpiece, you are more prone to present yourself as one and shine forth My glory. But when you neglect to cling to the truth about yourself, My child, then Satan lowers your estimation of yourself and you begin to live up to those low expectations.

I also want you to know today that when I created you, I formed you for a purpose. I have given you a unique blend of talents and limitations, experiences and limited frames of reference, personality enhancements and personality quirks—shall we say—to make you just the right person for specific tasks. I have lovingly wired your mind and heart and soul and body to do things no one other person could do or would even want to do. You are unique. Please relish that uniqueness and do not wrestle with it. It is your most distinct sign that you were creatively fashioned by a God who loves you.

Questions to ponder:
What are some of your more unique characteristics, both physical and personality traits?

What do you tend to like about yourself? What do you sometimes dislike about yourself?

How do you think God feels about those same things?

Additional scriptures to feast upon today:

Psalm 103:13-18
Psalm 139:13-16
Isaiah 49:5
Isaiah 64:8

As I swallow these scriptures, I am believing...

Day 15

But you are a chosen race, a royal priesthood, a holy nation, a people for God's own possession, that you may proclaim the excellencies of Him who has called you out of darkness into His marvelous light.
(1 Peter 2:9)

I want you to find significance in who you are and what I have gifted and called you to do. But I also want you to think even bigger than that. You see, you are a vital part of something bigger than just yourself.

You are a child in My family, an heir in My kingdom, a priest in My royal priesthood, a citizen in My holy nation. I value you and esteem the role you play in My work in this world.

Before, you were not a part of anything this big, important, eternal. You were simply living your own life, doing your own thing. But when you entered into covenant with Me, you became a vital part of the biggest thing there is.

I know that some days it does not seem as if you are doing anything of significance. But whether I have assigned you to take care of your children in the home or teach other peoples' children in the classroom, to coach little league teams or play soccer professionally, to sell pharmaceuticals or write prescriptions, to drill soldiers on the field or grill steaks in a restaurant, to write articles for a newspaper or write tickets for speeding motorists, I have called you to do your job well…because your work matters to Me.

Wherever you are carrying out your unique calling is your mission field, your ministry headquarters. It is an arena in which I have intentionally placed you for effectiveness and for My glory. When you treat that place and the tasks I have given you as some sort of default assignment, you diminish the significant work I have given you. But make no mistake, even if you do not see your significance in that place and in that work, I do. And I need you to see yourself in the same light as I do so you will respect the job enough to do it well.

You will lift the significance of your calling in your own estimation when you begin to cooperate with the bigger picture. Do you see how your assignments, regardless of what they might be, contribute to the larger goal? Do you recognize the need to be plugged into a local church so you might carry out your assignments with the aid, encouragement, and support of others who are on the same mission? Do you see that you have gifts, talents, experiences, and personality traits that can benefit them as they also work toward the greater goal?

Oh, precious child of Mine, take heart in the fact that you are part of something much bigger than yourself today. We have work to do and only you can do your assigned tasks.

Questions to ponder:
Have you considered what your current role is in the holy priesthood of the saints? What specific tasks has God called you to during this season of life?

What is it about being part of something bigger than ourselves that rings with significance? How does it make you feel to be a part of God's purposes on earth during this generation?

Additional scriptures to feast upon today:

Ephesians 2:10
Colossians 3:23-24
Titus 2:14
1 Peter 2:9-10

As I swallow these scriptures, I am believing...

Day 16

"'For I know the plans I have for you,' declares the Lord, 'plans for welfare and not for calamity to give you a future and a hope.'"
(Jeremiah 29:11)

I know there are times when you *feel* special and loved by Me, and there are times when you *feel* I am angry at you or, perhaps, simply not mindful of you. You are most prone to feel that you are insignificant to Me when either one of two things is going on: either you have drifted into defiant and willful sin or you are experiencing the consequences of sin, including My discipline.

Sweet child, when you choose to live contrary to My ways and Word, you will not *feel* close to Me. But I am still here, on My throne and in your heart, but not on the throne *of* your heart. Unfortunately, your ungodly actions have a way of drowning out My already quiet voice. If you choose to walk your own way, you will certainly feel as if you have left Me far behind. But I am, in fact, following after you, pursuing you, drawing you back to Me. That is how significant you are to Me. And when you finally turn around (and that is always required—that turning around), you will find Me right there with open arms, ready to pull you in close and secure once again.

You also may feel far from Me when I am allowing the consequences of your sin to press hard upon you. You may feel like the unfavored stepchild at those times. But, truthfully, I only discipline those who are My legitimate children. You bear My name, you have been granted My inheritance, and you have been called into the family business of redeeming souls. I have much riding on you and I will not allow you to live like a spoiled rich kid, squandering all you have been given. So yes, I do discipline you. I chasten those I love.

But you can know this truth, sweet one: I am the perfect and loving disciplinarian. I only and always discipline effectively. In other words, I will never be heavy-handed or unreasonable with you. I will only discipline you in a way that produces good results in your life. I do not shame or injure or destroy or belittle when I discipline My children. My goal is always to bring about good in your life, even taking the mess you have created with your sinful actions or words and turning that mess into something beautiful with time. That is called redemption. I will always redeem what you have lost with your wayward living if you will allow Me. There may be a little pain in the process, and you may not *feel* as if you are in My good graces, but I am counting on you to remember the truth: I discipline those whom I love because they are eternally important to Me. *You* are eternally important to Me.

Questions to ponder:
When do you feel the furthest from God? Why?

How will it help you to face God's disciplinary measures in your life if you remember that He only disciplines those whom He loves and calls His children?

Additional scriptures to feast upon today:

Proverbs 3:11-12
Jeremiah 29:11-14
Lamentations 3:22-23
Hebrews 12:5-11

As I swallow these scriptures, I am believing…

Day 17

And let the favor of the Lord our God be upon us;
And do confirm for us the work of our hands;
Yes, confirm the work of our hands.
(Psalm 90:17)

Are you ready for your assignments today? Are you anticipating doing great things? Are you prepared—mind, body and soul?

I have significant work for you today. You may wonder how that can be, depending on your plans for this day. But whether you are cleaning your home or cleaning up a manuscript, wiping runny noses or wiping math problems off a white board, singing finger-play songs with preschoolers or singing anthems in your church choir, cutting the grass in your backyard or cutting fine wisps of hair off the head of a whimpering two-year-old, you have something important to do this day.

Part of the significance of your task is the work itself. I want you to bake deliciously, cut straight, lead enthusiastically, teach with clarity, mother tenderly, patrol diligently, or paint beautifully. I call you to be alert, bring your "A" game, apply some elbow grease, put in the time, and finish strong. People are watching, you know. Oh, I am sure there are days, perhaps many days, when you feel as if no one notices what you've done. No one compliments your work, thanks you for serving, or rewards your diligence. But trust Me, they see. They see the big picture. They notice your work ethic, your energy, your level of commitment, your integrity.

And every time someone forms an opinion about you and your work, they are also forming an opinion about Me and My work. You see, many people know you are linked to Me. They know you know Me, you worship Me, you call yourself by My name. So your work, all of it, is a reflection upon Me. Do it well.

But I also call you to be on the alert for how I am at work around you as you fulfill your assignments. You might notice Me speaking to the hearts of your students, co-workers, customers, family members, patients or clients. They may have questions about Me which you can answer, misconceptions you can clear up with Scripture, frustrations you can help them pray about, fears you can settle with truth, tears you can wipe away with My compassion, offenses you can overcome with My mercy, and accusations you can handle with My grace. In fact, every time you interact with another person—whether by telephone, Internet, the written word or in person—you have the opportunity to represent Me. You are My ambassador today, and you have multiple crucial and significant assignments. Are you ready?

Questions to ponder:
What are the specific work assignments you have today? Have you asked God to "confirm" or give significance to them? Why don't you do that now?

Have you noticed God at work in your work environment recently? If so, ask Him how you might join Him today in that work. If not, ask Him to open your eyes to where He is at work so you can be of assistance to Him as He leads.

Additional scriptures to feast upon today:

Matthew 5:16
Galatians 6:9-10
Ephesians 4:1-3
Philippians 2:14-16
Colossians 3:23-24

As I swallow these scriptures, I am believing...

Day 18

By this we know that we abide in Him and He in us, because He has given us of His Spirit.
(1 John 4:13)

You live in a dark world. While you still traverse the sod of earth, you are surrounded by darkness. Most of the people of the world, people whom I love and died for, live in darkness.

When I was born of a woman and lived among man, My light came into the world. For the first time ever, there was more than just a glimpse of My light here or there. I shone brightly into a dark world with My full brilliance. Many were offended by My light. They did not recognize Me nor embrace Me. But you have walked into My light. You are now a child of light.

When I ascended into Heaven to sit at the right hand of My Father, I promised My disciples to send another…another light…One who would illuminate, guide, and comfort…One who would shine My light into the dark world. The Holy Spirit, My Spirit, came into the world to take up residency in men and women who have received Me as their Savior and committed to Me as their Lord. If you are My child, My follower, My disciple, then you are indwelt by the Holy Spirit, My Spirit, the Spirit of the Living God, the light of the world.

You are My light bearer. You are My ambassador of light and life. With My very Spirit within you, you are now one who must share My Gospel with a world of people who live in darkness. Without your participation, who will go? Who will share? Who will shine the light?

You have died to your fleshly nature and have willingly given My Holy Spirit control of your life. To the degree that you actually yield to the Spirit's direction each day, you live a life that reflects His nature, My nature. You show the world uncanny, divine, and supernatural love, joy, peace, patience, kindness, goodness, faithfulness, gentleness, and self-control, the likes of which the world has never seen elsewhere. That is the potential you carry about in you every day. And with that potential, I have given you the most important mission in the world—the ministry of reconciling lost and hopeless people to Me, their Creator and God.

One day I will come again and take you home with Me. I will remove you and all My other followers from this earth. On that day, the light will go out. There will be no light bearers in the world and people will struggle as they have never struggled before. But until that day, I ask you to sit up, better yet, stand up and heed the significance of your presence in this world. You are My light bearer. Let My light shine!

Questions to ponder:

How does it give you significance to realize you and other believers just like you are the source of God's light in this dark world?

How well is God's light shining through your life? What might you need to do so that His light can shine more brightly through you?

Additional scriptures to feast upon today:

John 1:4-5, 9-14
2 Corinthians 4:5-7
2 Corinthians 5:17-21
Ephesians 5:8
1 John 2:20

As I swallow these scriptures, I am believing...

Day 19

But by the grace of God I am what I am, and His grace toward me did not prove vain; but I labored even more than all of them, yet not I, but the grace of God with me.
(1 Corinthians 15:10)

Your self-worth does not rest on what you can accomplish or become. It rests upon My work *in* you. That's right; I am at work *in you.* In fact, that is where I do most of My work these days—in the lives of men and women, boys and girls. While you can certainly see Me at work *around* you—in nature, in governments, in churches, etc.—you need to understand that I have moved My "headquarters," so to speak, to the inside.

Do you really comprehend the truth of "Christ in you"? In years past, people saw My work predominantly through very visible and external manifestations of My power. When I walked the earth before ascending into heaven, I was most often known for and sought after for external miracles such as healing physical illnesses, calming storms, turning water into wine and feeding hungry bellies. But this side of the cross of Calvary, I am most intently at work in hearts, minds, and souls. I am changing lives from the inside out. And a changed life is the best kind of miracle, is it not?

What does that mean for you? It means that My indwelling, transformational, intentional, and powerful work *in you* is a priority to Me. I have begun a good work in you. It is not a cookie cutter work; it is a very specific, personal work. I repeat; I have begun something awesome and inherently *good* in you. I have a plan for My work in you; it is not hit-and-miss. I know what good things I am working to accomplish, and I will complete the good work I have begun. You can count on Me.

It is My plan for you to be able to look back on the recent years of your life and notice some supernatural changes. Have you stopped lately to consider from whence you came? Have you looked back over your shoulder long enough to contemplate My grace at work in your life? Do you see how far I have brought you already? You might want to spend some time reflecting on those things today.

When you pause to realize that I have indeed been at work in your life, that I am doing amazing things in you and through you, and that I am busy even now, I hope those realizations will give you reason to think more highly of yourself, to see how truly important you are to Me. No, I do not want you to think more highly of yourself than you should. But I do want you to have a healthy self-esteem based largely on the fact that the same God who spoke the world into existence, brought His people out of bondage, fed His children with daily manna, calmed the waves and the wind, turned water into wine, healed the leper and the blind man, and ultimately conquered sin and death—that God is graciously and intentionally at work inside of you…today.

Questions to ponder:
Why does it increase your sense of worth when you realize God is at work in you?

Name several things you have seen God do over time *in* you, not *around* you or *for* you, but *in* you.

Additional scriptures to feast upon today:

Psalm 66:16
Romans 12:1-3
Philippians 1:6
Philippians 2:13

As I swallow these scriptures, I am believing...

Day 20

All Scripture is inspired by God and profitable for teaching, for reproof, for correction, for training in righteousness; that the man of God may be adequate, equipped for every good work.
(2 Timothy 3:16-17)

Do you realize what a treasure you have? Not only do you have access to it, but you have the key to unlock it. You have the insider scoop on the most important information in the world—counsel, wisdom, direction, truth. Most of the world is struggling along without these navigation tools, while many seek to find the answers they long for in all the wrong places. You, on the other hand, have My Word in your possession and the ability gradually and increasingly to comprehend it with the supernatural assistance of My indwelling Spirit.

At no other time in history have people had such access to My holy, infallible, trustworthy, and supernaturally powerful Word. Even in recent centuries, believers were completely dependent upon the teaching and interpretations of man in order to learn from Me. But you probably have more than one Bible in your home. It is in your language, relatively inexpensive, easily accessible, and well bound with notes, cross references, and other study helps.

Do you recognize the divine treasure you hold? It is not just another good book; it is *The* Book. It is alive and able to penetrate the toughest heart, change the hardest mind, and save the most despondent soul. It does not go out and return to Me without accomplishing that for which I have sent it out.

I have entrusted you, in this generation, with ready access to My Word. You have at your fingertips the words of hope for hopeless times, encouragement for when all seems lost, truth for when life seems gray, and wisdom for every decision. I do not remind you of this treasure simply to put a smug smile on your face, however. I impress upon you the wealth you possess so you will gladly, willingly, and passionately share it with the people around you. People want a manual for living, and you have it in your possession.

I am all too aware that the prince of this world has worked fervently to make My followers feel like duds. That's right, duds. He has convinced too many of you that you are square, simple-minded, unsophisticated, and silly for embracing My Word. But while the gospel, My good news, may appear simple and foolish to many, it is in fact My power for salvation to everyone who believes. Guard, with all diligence, the treasure which has been entrusted to you and proclaim it with confidence and enthusiasm.

Questions to ponder:
What do you love most about the Word of God? Why is it precious to you?

How does remembering the treasure you possess in God's Word increase your sense of significance?

How does owning, reading, and meditating upon the Word of God make you a significant player in this world?

Additional scriptures to feast upon today:

Deuteronomy 8:3
Psalm 119:105
John 1:1
John 8:31-32
Hebrews 4:12

As I swallow these scriptures, I am believing...

Day 21

Humble yourself in the presence of the Lord, and He will exalt you. (James 4:10)

Do you sometimes long to win, be first, get the applause, wear the crown, or hear your name called out from the platform? Seeking a little glory for yourself or craving the spotlight is only human.

But those desires find their root in an offensive little thing called pride. While pride—that desire for self-exaltation—causes all manner of sins from covetousness to murder, from exaggeration to stealing, it always includes the misconception that you somehow *deserve* to be treated better. And one of the reasons you believe you deserve better treatment from others is that you discount *My* treatment of you.

Today I ask you to humble yourself in My presence so that *I* can exalt you at the right time. And when I exalt you—lift your chin and raise your gaze, put an eternal crown of glory on your sweet little head, dress you in a fresh, clean garment of costly linen, and speak blessings over you—you will be exalted indeed.

When other people count you as most popular, most talented, best mom, favorite teacher, most productive employee, or exceptionally beautiful, they are making judgment calls based on external and fading glory. As fun and flattering as those accolades may be (and mostly harmless, as long as you take them in stride), they actually mean nothing in My economy. And you need to remember that next year or maybe even next week someone else will be the favorite, the winner.

But when I exalt you, My criteria for calling you out are My esteem for you and your esteem for Me, nothing more. I already esteem you highly. You are precious to Me and nothing can make you more or less in My sight. But we, you and I, are still in the process of working on your estimation of Me. I want you to see that I am God and you are not. I want you to depend on Me for every little thing, not because I am trying to keep you under My thumb. I do not have a fragile ego as some would think. But I long to provide every good and perfect gift for you out of love…including a winning moment here and there.

Would you like to know the true secret to exaltation? Would you like to know what it really takes to be a winner? It will sound like such a foreign concept compared to the world's mantra of "just go for it," but in My kingdom—the one where it really counts—the path to the seat of honor is through the servant's entrance. I am quite sure you have heard that before, but I am asking you to fasten that truth to your soul today. You bow low enough to serve others and I, the King of kings and Lord of lords, will exalt you when it really matters.

Questions to ponder:
What are you craving recognition for right now? Have you talked to God about it?

How could you humble yourself in God's presence and serve someone else instead of clamoring for exaltation today?

Additional scriptures to feast upon today:

Proverbs 29:23
Matthew 20:26-28
Matthew 23:12
Luke 14:11

As I swallow these scriptures, I am believing...

Day 22

What is man, that Thou dost take thought of him?
And the son of man, that Thou dost care for him?
(Psalm 8:4)

Bless you. That's right, I bless you. Do you grasp the significance of My blessing? When I bless you, I am speaking good into your life. When I bless you, I am giving you good. When I bless you, I am doing you well. When I bless you, I am standing you upright, firmly establishing you, and sending you out into the world with an anointing of honor and purpose.

Everyone craves a blessing from those they love and esteem. It is normal to want to be blessed by your parents, your spouse, your employer, your mentors, or others who are significant to you. And it may be that time has passed and your desire for a blessing has been overlooked, ignored or even rejected by someone from whom you desired a good word. Is that true for you? Do you feel as if you can never measure up, never please enough to hear the words of blessing from someone significant to you?

Maybe you have even been cursed. Perhaps someone in your past or even with whom you relate on a daily basis has not only refused to bless you with good, but that person has cursed you with negative words, harmful prophesies over your life, scowls of rejection, or simple neglect. Beloved, I will bring those who have hurt you to justice. Leave justice to Me. But, meanwhile, I ask you to turn your discouraged and broken heart to Me and listen to My voice.

These are some of My blessings for you:

- You are beautiful.
- You are loved.
- You are important.
- You are able.
- You are gifted.
- You are completely forgiven, clean.
- You can do *all things* when I provide the strength.
- You have important work to do for Me.
- You are a new person; you are not the same person you used to be.
- I am for you.

I bless you. If you have missed the blessing of someone in your life, I ask you to entrust that void to Me from this point on and relish My blessing instead. And if you have received multiple blessings from people in your life, I encourage you to enjoy those, but put them in proper perspective and crave My blessing in your life more than any other. Seek My blessing. I gladly bless you.

Questions to ponder:
Is there someone in your life from whom you have wanted a blessing but have never felt as if you received one? Who?

What are some of the ways in which you see God's blessing in your life?

What will seeking God's blessing above the blessings of people look like in your life?

Additional scriptures to feast upon today:

Genesis 5:1-2
1 Chronicles 4:9-10
Psalm 40:4
Psalm 144:15
Ephesians 1:3

As I swallow these scriptures, I am believing…

When you are grieving and you need someone to sympathize with you as well as give you comfort, support, and encouragement...

He heals the brokenhearted,
And binds up their sorrows.
Psalm 147:3

Day 23

He heals the brokenhearted,
And binds up their sorrows.
(Psalm 147:3)

I see your pain and know your sorrow. I feel your grief and comprehend the depth of your losses. Trust Me; I grieve, too. I grieve for many of the same reasons you do.

I have been rejected, cursed, misunderstood, and mocked. I have wept both for my own loss as well as the painful sorrows of those I love. In fact, your losses are My losses. I have said goodbye to those I love, those for whom I died. I have loved with a passionate and tender love only to have My love refused and thrown back at Me. And I (the Father) have watched My beloved Son die a painful death. I am fully acquainted with sorrow and I know how it breaks your heart.

I treasure your tears. They are not lost on Me, but instead they are precious to Me. If you will allow Me, I can gently wipe them away and replace them with joy. I want to walk beside you in your grief, giving you time and strength and comfort and everything else you need to regain your composure. Then I want to give you a greater joy than you ever knew before.

Hand me your broken heart, all the pieces. I will not just put it back together, but I will completely heal it. I will bind up your wounds and make you whole. I will restore your peace, your joy, and your hope. Right now, you may be marked by the ashes of mourning, but one day soon I will replace those ashes with a garland of joy. Right now, you may mourn, but one day you will again be glad. And right now, you may feel as if you are about to faint from the constant pain in your heart, but one day soon you will again have the strength and passion to sing praises. At that point, people will look at you and be amazed at the transformation. In fact, you may look in the mirror and be amazed because where once you saw someone who was sad and despondent, you will then see a more formidable person, one who has stood strong through the difficult times and now is in full bloom again. There is a time to mourn, but there is also a time to dance again.

Please know that I love you, that I am mindful of your deep sorrow, and that I care. While others will have to return to their lives and cannot be with you and share your pain every moment, I will never leave you. I am right here in your presence, holding you, loving you, weeping with you, and feeling your grief.

One day soon I will wipe away the last tears and there will be no more. There will be no more sorrow, pain, or grief. And I promise you the dancing will never end.

Questions to ponder:
Are you mourning over a loss of any sort right now? What are you grieving over?

What do you need to remember about Jesus today that will help you survive this day and thrive again one day soon?

If you are not grieving, do you know someone who is? How might they benefit from you sharing these promises with them?

Additional scriptures to feast upon today:

Genesis 16:1-13
Psalm 23:4
Psalm 56:8
Psalm 116:15
Isaiah 61:1-3
Matthew 5:4
John 11:33-35
Revelation 21:3-4

As I swallow these scriptures, I am believing…

When you just need a friend and some sweet companionship...

Jesus has chosen you to be His friend.
John 15:16

Day 24

"Greater love has no one than this, that one lay down his life for his friends."
(John 15:13)

I have been a friend to you. I have laid down my life for you, died for you, My friend. I have chosen to call you friend. And I have done everything necessary for us to be friends, sweet companions.

But you need to choose to be My friend. If you would rather be friends with the world, then we cannot be friends. So if you choose to blend in with the world, take on the ideals of this world, spend your time on the pursuits of this world, and buddy up to the values of this world, then we will not be on friendly terms. In fact, you put yourself in direct opposition to Me and My purposes when you befriend the world. It is your decision.

If you choose to be My friend—and it is always your choice—then I offer you the sweetest of friendships. I will be your constant companion, and yet I will never push Myself on you. I will listen to your every word intently, offering My wisdom and guidance only when you ask for it or are in a frame of mind for receiving it. I will weep when you weep and laugh when you laugh. I will keep your confidences, value your feelings, allow you to be who you were created to be, and encourage you to be all you are meant to be.

And this is a two-way street. If we are friends, you and I, then I will disclose My secrets to you. I will let you in on what

I am doing around you. You will begin to notice what I am up to and where I am headed. And I will not allow you to feel like an outsider. No, I will include you. I'll ask you to join Me on important missions, bring you along on exciting journeys and invite you to extravagant celebrations. I will even provide you back stage seats to some of the most incredible, memorable and fascinating events you could ever witness. You will see Me change peoples' lives, work in ways you would never expect, and even do a few special miracles just for you. You will honestly begin to know that we are intimately acquainted and that you are precious to Me. I will be your sweet companion, an engaged and fully interested witness to every moment of your life. And you will be a witness of My activity around you as well. And here is something else you need to know. Our relationship, yours and Mine, will be unique—just as unique as you are from everyone else on the planet. Just as I have had unique relationships with My friends Moses, Abraham, and Peter, I will reserve a special bond for you and Me, My precious friend.

If you desire to be My friend, treat Me like a friend. Talk to Me, share your dreams and hopes and hurts with Me, spend time with Me, and anticipate Me doing the same with you. I love you, My dear friend.

Questions to ponder:

What characteristics do you look for in a friend? How does Jesus fit the bill?

How could you be a better friend to Jesus?

Additional scriptures to feast upon today:

Psalm 4:3
Psalm 25:14
John 15:13-16
James 2:23

As I swallow these scriptures, I am believing...

When you long to be noticed and favored by someone...

Jesus picks you out of the crowd, speaks directly to you, and promises you your heart's desires.
John 4:5-26

Day 25

I will sing to the Lord,
Because He has dealt bountifully with me.
(Psalm 13:6)

You have found favor in My sight. Do you understand what that means? It does not mean you have jumped through enough hoops or stood out in the crowd with wild and silly antics in order to catch My attention. I am not so easily impressed. Nor, however, am I prone to requiring from you preposterous antics in order to please Me. Instead, I am constantly searching for those who simply have a heart for the things which really matter to Me. And when I find such a person, I graciously grant them My favor.

When you take time to sit at My feet and read My Word, I am pleased, and I respond by granting you My favor. When you seek to have your soul desires met at My table, I am thrilled to serve you hearty and satisfying portions. And when you call upon Me for wisdom, discernment and guidance, I know that you are serious about following Me, so I am quick to hold out My hand to you, guide you, and walk with you. I am even more than willing to stoop down when you are at your lowest and set you back on your feet with a gentle touch. Why? Not because you have impressed Me as you might endeavor to impress people with flattering words, showy behavior, a sparkling personality or groomed beauty, but because your heart is quietly and steadfastly set upon Me. Keep it there.

It is common for people to seek favor from one another. People want to be popular, liked, highly esteemed, catered to, and adored. But the things which gain you favor with other people will not work with Me. I see through the eager antics. I see past the flattering words. And I know who you really are behind your smooth performance, your generous gestures, and your polished appearance. I am looking at your heart. And when I see that your heart is focused on Me and the things I am passionate about, you receive My brand of favor.

Here is the really good news I want to convey to you: You do not have to work so hard with Me. You do not have to perform, keep up appearances, or polish your presentation. You simply have to stay focused…on Me.

Are you in a situation today where you need to hear a little applause, receive some affirmation or even wear the "most favored" badge? Stop looking to others for those things. Instead, allow Me to show you the favor of the King of kings. You love me with all your heart, mind, body, and soul, and I will make sure you know "you have found favor with God." You will hear My applause loud and clear.

Questions to ponder:
What types of things do you normally do to acquire the favor of other people?

How can you resist the trap of people-pleasing by remembering that Jesus offers you His favor through much more reasonable means?

Have you asked Jesus for His favor recently? It's quite ok to do that, you know…

Additional scriptures to feast upon today:

Psalm 119:58
Psalm 147:11
Proverbs 22:1
Daniel 9:13, 19-23

As I swallow these scriptures, I am believing…

When you are carrying the weight of guilt and you desperately need relief...

Jesus washes you thoroughly from your iniquity and cleanses you completely from your sin.
Psalm 51:2

Day 26

I acknowledged my sin to Thee, and my iniquity I did not hide;
I said, "I will confess my transgressions to the Lord";
and Thou didst forgive the guilt of my sin.
(Psalm 32:5)

Are you wearing the heavy, uncomfortable cloak of shame? Do you feel like your past mistakes are emblazoned upon your chest like a scarlet letter A? Oh, My child, you are imagining things, thanks to the mind games of the enemy. You have been duped into carrying around guilt you do not own. He may have even convinced you that carrying that burdensome load is some sort of penance prescribed by Me for your sins. He is wrong; do not listen to him. And if you are still feeling even one twinge of guilt from sins that have been covered by My blood, then you are serving unnecessary time for an excused charge. It's time to come out of that prison once and for all.

So many of My precious children continue to pay penance for sins I have already cast into the deepest sea. Or at least they continue to see themselves defined by those sinful acts. Do you see yourself as a liar, an adulteress, a gossip, an addict, or the perpetrator of any other kind of sin? Unless you continue to live in that sin, you are not to take on that mantle. When you do, you subtly convince yourself that you are capable of nothing better, that you cannot help yourself, that you will never be free of the temptations that beckon you, and that you can never be pleasing in My sight. And that, sadly, keeps you from coming to Me freely and often.

But dear child, you stand completely clean in My sight. And let's not cheapen that gift. You see, that does not mean I have glossed over your faults and mistakes as some people may have. I have not winked at them and glibly excused them. No, I have died for them. I carried them all to the cross and died with the weight of them on My guiltless shoulders. And now you are clean.

So here is what I want you to do. I want you to see that you are brand new in My eyes. You are a new creature. I have given you a new heart, a new spirit, and My Spirit to enable you to live a new kind of life. The sins of your past—ten years ago, three months ago, yesterday—are gone. I do not recall them. I want you to stop recalling them, too.

Instead, I call you to live as a free person. I call you to cast away the cloak of shame and pick up the garment of rejoicing. And when you feel those prison doors slamming shut on you again, realize it is the enemy's lies that have put you behind them. But he has no locks on those iron doors. I have set you free. Run free.

Questions to ponder:
What guilt weighs you down?

What difference does it make in your ability to live a God-pleasing life to know your sins have completely been forgiven and cast away from you as far as the east is from the west?

Do you really believe that you are now guilt free?

Additional scriptures to feast upon today:

Psalm 103:10-12
2 Corinthians 5:17
Hebrews 10:19-22
1 John 1:9

As I swallow these scriptures, I am believing...

When you feel like everything around you is falling apart or out of your hands and you desire to regain a sense of control...

Jesus calls you to trust in His lovingkindness.
Psalm 13:5

Day 27

Cease striving and know that I am God.
(Psalm 46:10a)

Rest assured. I am in control.

Sometimes My children wrestle with their circumstances or even with other people because they feel an unquenchable need to be in control. Do you sometimes feel that way? Do you feel like you know what is best or ideal, whether for yourself, someone you love, your church, or some organization of which you are a part? Maybe you even feel that you know My will in a certain situation, and you are frustrated because someone else is not cooperating with the plan.

Child, I appreciate your desire to see My will carried out, if that is indeed your motivation. But you can trust Me to oversee My will. If I have plans, I will accomplish them. And no person, thing or force will thwart My hand. I will see My purposes through.

So I ask you instead to rest. Do not rest on your own understanding of the situation. Do not even spend time trying to figure out how I am going to move things from point A to point B. That is My concern alone. No, just rest in Me. Quit striving, working, scheming, mulling things over or arranging things.

Sometimes My children desire to control things or other people because they lack personal control. I ask you to stop trying to control any other person or situation, and instead allow Me to give you the grace gift of self-control. You will undoubtedly have difficulty trying to control your own speech, facial expressions, body language, temper, or behavior if you try to manage things on your own, especially if you are in a situation that feels out of control to you. Let's face it; sometimes in your passionate desire to control others, you lose your own. But if you allow My Spirit, which indwells the believer, to take over and call the shots, you will be amazed at how you can indeed practice self-control. Yield to My gentle, quiet voice when I ask you to hold your tongue, maintain your composure, walk away from the situation, put the phone down, or leave something or someone alone. You just concentrate on pleasing Me by obeying the standards and precepts I have set out for you in My Word. Then, as you cooperate with My Spirit by yielding to Me, I will be able to work even more quickly and efficiently in not only the people around you, but in you. I am at work. You can count on it. So you can stop striving and just rest. Do you trust Me?

Questions to ponder:
What or whom have you been trying to control recently? Honestly consider why you feel you need to control this situation.

What can you do to relinquish control to God in this area today?

On what truth do you need to meditate in order to quench this desire for control?

Additional scriptures to feast upon today:

Job 23:13
Psalm 52:7-9
Psalm 13:5
Proverbs 3:5-8

As I swallow these scriptures, I am believing...

When you desperately need wisdom...

Jesus promises to provide it generously and without reproach.
James 1:5

Day 28

I will instruct you and teach you in the way which you should go;
I will counsel you with My eye upon you.
(Psalm 32:8)

There are few things nobler to be desired than wisdom. And I long to give you wisdom for living. To have wisdom is to have My perspective on your situations and on life. It is to see your dilemmas, goals, conflicts, pursuits, relationships, and ideas from My vantage point. It is to see the world clearly and to esteem only that which I declare eternally significant, while putting aside that which I deem unworthy of your pursuit. I want you to want wisdom, and I will generously give it if you ask with faith.

But here's the thing about attaining wisdom. You must seek it. I must see that you are seriously devoted to seeing things from My perspective. There are many provisions I simply shower upon My creation as I will, both the righteous and the unrighteous: breath, days of life, talents, happy moments. There are other gifts I have reserved for those who have chosen to be My children, but I generously offer them with an open hand. They are simply there for the taking: hope, spiritual gifts for service, My protection, My presence, physical provision. And then there is wisdom.

To receive wisdom, you must show by your attitude of reverence that you understand who I am and who you are in relationship to Me. You must admit that I have something you do not have and that you need it desperately. I hold wisdom in a closed hand and offer it only to those who seek it with a voracious appetite.

I have stated in My Word that fearing Me is the beginning of wisdom. But you want to do more than *begin* to have wisdom. So you must dedicate yourself to seeking it. Do not be distracted by the savvy sounding philosophers of this world, the newest theories, or the popular psychology. Let Me warn you; they will sound wise. But the wisdom of this world is really just sophisticated foolishness. Steer clear of it. Instead, come to Me for understanding, discernment, and guidance. You will not necessarily become wiser just by spending much time in My Word, although familiarity with and meditation on My Word are definitely required to have My perspective. Nor will you find wisdom just by reading or studying My Word. You must seek *Me* and ask *Me* for wisdom.

How will you know when you have received wisdom from Me? First of all, My wisdom is pure. It isn't a culturally accepted and trendy blend of the world's philosophies and My Word. It is starkly different from the world's viewpoint. Second, My wisdom always calls for you to respond to other people, your situation, or Me with a consistent character marked by peace, gentleness, respectful cooperation, mercy and goodness. My wisdom will never call for you to react contrary to My character.

Come to Me and I will make you wise for living.

Questions to ponder:
For what do you desperately need wisdom right now?

What are some ways you have been trying to attain wisdom?

How will you know godly wisdom when you see it?

Additional scriptures to feast upon today:

Job 28:12-13, 28
Psalm 51:6
Ecclesiastes 7:11-12
1 Corinthians 1:20-25
James 3:17

As I swallow these scriptures, I am believing…

When you are blue and you long to have joy deep down in your soul...

Jesus promises joy in His presence.
Psalm 16:11

Day 29

Then I will go to the altar of God,
To God my exceeding joy;
And upon the lyre I shall praise Thee, O God, my God.
(Psalm 43:4)

You are My joy. It was for the thrilling joy of bringing you into relationship with My Father that I endured the cross and the weight of your sin. I have been through pain, rejection, loss, and death while still keeping My joy before Me. Because of the joy that lay ahead, I was able to bear all things. I so wanted you to be in a sweet and thriving relationship with Me. And now that you have been redeemed, I smile over you constantly. You give *Me* great joy.

Do you feel My joy? You can. But if you allow your gaze to turn to the cares of this world—the disappointments and challenges—then you will be prone to losing your joy. Instead, do as I did on My way to the cross. Keep focused on Me, your true source of joy.

Come and spend time with Me. Acknowledge who I am, My character and ways. *You will find joy in My presence.* Take refuge in my strong arms. *You will find joy in My strength and protection.* Take notice of My works. Look around you and see the evidences of My activity. *You will find joy in My awesome works.* Seek to stay in a right relationship with Me by walking in My ways and repenting when you fall out of step. *You will find joy in My grace and forgiveness.* Rest in My trustworthiness and allow Me to provide faithfully for you all that you need. *You will find joy in my faithful provision.* Run to Me when you are in trouble and the waves of anxiety are crashing in. *You will find joy in My deliverance.*

Keep in mind that joy is not the same as happiness. Joy, My child, is so much more sustaining and goes much deeper than simple happiness. Joy is an overwhelming combination of things that only I can truly provide you on a consistent basis: peace, hope, security, love, and a clear conscience. When you have these things and you are in a right relationship with your Creator, you will have uncontainable joy despite the ups and downs of life. You will feel joyful because all is assuredly well with your soul.

No one else can give you such security of soul. Nothing else can produce such feelings of bliss. But when you draw close to Me, look fully into My face, and put your trust in Me, you will find that you have deep and abiding joy, overflowing and ecstatic joy. And when your soul is full because I have graciously provided all you long for in a healthy and sustaining way, joy will bubble up in your life like a rushing fountain of clear, clean water. It is My great pleasure to give you an abundant, joyful life!

Questions to ponder:
What does it feel like to you to have joy?

What are some of the characteristics of Jesus that give you great joy?

Additional scriptures to feast upon today:

1 Chronicles 16:27
Psalm 16:11
Psalm 21:6
Psalm 89:15
Philippians 4:4

As I swallow these scriptures, I am believing…

When you feel overwhelmed by the demands of life and you desperately crave strength...

Jesus will infuse you with His strength.
Philippians 4:13

Day 30

Your God has commanded your strength;
Show Thyself strong, O God, who hast acted on our behalf.
(Psalm 68:28)

As long as you walk on this earth, you will grow weary at times. Life here is difficult, draining. One day you will rest in My full glory and you will never tire again, but until then, I promise to provide the strength and renewal you need to finish the course.

Before the demands of life have the opportunity to sap you of your strength and drain you so dry that you have nothing left to sustain you, I ask you to come to Me. Do not wait until you have poured out every last ounce of My life-sustaining power before you turn to me with your empty cup. Instead, make it a habit of gaining nourishment from Me every day. Spend time seeking your soul's desires from Me, and I will cause you to be like a spring-fed garden whose source of refreshment never ceases to flow. And in the garden of your well-watered life, others will find beauty, refuge, bounty, and respite from life's harsh treatment. Won't that be a joy? Oh, do not worry about them draining you when they find sweet refreshment within the circumference of your life. If you are pouring out with love and generosity to others that which I have given to you, I will make sure you are replenished and full.

But when some suddenly draining circumstance slings you to the ground with exhaustion, or a sustained season of giving yourself to others causes you slowly to lose your steam, run to Me, dear one. I will not hold you in contempt for being tired and spent. Instead, as I did for My servant Elijah, I will nurse you back to full strength by feeding you My daily bread: truth. Then I will allow you to rest comfortably in the shelter of My compassion and set your feet firmly back on solid ground.

If I give you an especially daunting assignment, I promise also to provide you the supernatural strength to handle it. But if you step out on your own, then you are on your own. Instead, do not try to accomplish anything in the strength of your own flesh. Pour out before Me anything you might be inclined to handle on your own. Drain out your pride, your manmade plans, your superficial coping devices. Then, empty and poured out, turn to Me. I will not pour My divine strength into a vessel that is already filled with self-determination, self-motivation, or willpower. But I will generously infuse with resurrection power the one who is broken and spilled out. Your weakness will serve as the perfect container for My strength. And as I command My strength to come upon you, you will rise with eagles' wings and soar above your circumstances. I will give you the strength you need and more.

Questions to ponder:
What life circumstances drain you the most of your stamina and strength?

Describe the characteristics of a life that looks and feels like a well-watered garden.

Additional scriptures to feast upon today:

Psalm 68:34-35
Psalm 138:3
Isaiah 40:28-31
Isaiah 58:10-11

As I swallow these scriptures, I am believing...

When your soul is restless
and hungry for that
elusive something...

Jesus will always provide
bountifully.
Psalm 116:7

Day 31

Lord, all my desire is before Thee;
And my sighing is not hidden from Thee.
(Psalm 38:9)

Oh precious child, do not think for one minute that I am unfamiliar with the restlessness in your soul. Do not assume it is something you need to hide from Me with shame. Yes, I can completely satisfy your soul with good things. And it is also true that nothing and no one besides Me can meet your needs in such an enduring, healthy, and satisfying way. But hear Me on this: You will continue to have days when you do not *feel* satisfied, when your soul yearns for something you cannot even put your finger on. You will occasionally feel a restless urge to pursue something more, to go further. You will experience a gnawing and inexplicable hunger at times.

The enemy would have you believe that these hunger pangs prove I cannot satisfy your soul's every desire. He would try to convince you that you are missing out, that there is something more, that I am holding something back from you. And then, with suspicion and unrest planted in your mind, he would have you go on an unfruitful and dangerous search for that elusive something.

Instead, I ask you to come to Me with every soul desire you experience, even when you cannot name that for which you hunger. Just come and tell Me plainly that you are hungry. I, the One who knows you intimately and thoroughly, the One who created you with every soul hunger you have, and the One who loves you dearly, can interpret the grumblings of your hungry soul without any effort. And, even if you can never name the thing for which you long, I will satisfy your thirsty soul and fill your hungry soul with what is good through and through.

And allow Me to fill you in on one more important truth. Until you see Me face to face and live forever in the shadow of My glory, you will hunger. That hunger is the healthy longing that draws you back to Me every day and keeps you restless and uncomfortable in a world for which you are not intended. You are not a citizen of this world in which you now live. You, My precious child, are hungry for home. Do you feel it? Do you recognize that sustained longing for a permanent and safe place to rest your head, to lay down your cares, and to breathe with relief? You want to go home. Oh, it may not be time yet and you may not be ready yet. But one day I will come and take you home. And then, My precious child, in the presence of the One who loves you like no other, you will be completely satisfied…at last.

Questions to ponder:
Do you ever have an inexplicable hunger in your soul? What does it feel like in you?

What difference will it make in the future to turn that restless hunger toward eternity?

Additional scriptures to feast upon today:

Psalm 17:15
Psalm 63:1, 5
Psalm 107:8-9
Philippians 3:20
Revelation 22:14, 17

As I swallow these scriptures, I am believing...

Savor the Satisfaction

It is my hope that over the past 31 days you have become more convinced than ever that Jesus, the bread of life, can truly satisfy your soul's every desire. Yes, God gives most of us many additional blessings that thrill our souls. And we need to see those gifts as coming from the hand of God and enjoy them fully.

It is perfectly acceptable and even wise to engage in your relationships fully, depend on people, and even need what they have to offer. But be wary of demanding or expecting from them what only God can give consistently and abundantly.

It is also normal and healthy to enjoy the things God blesses you with—your home, good food, and other possessions. But be careful of running to any of these things or others in order to fill your soul's deepest desires. Resist the temptation to worship the gift rather than the Giver of all good and perfect gifts. That tendency is a snare to which many of us have fallen victim, and it often leads to addictions we later regret.

Finally, we all have been blessed with experiences we enjoy and gain from. Whether you love travelling, excelling at your job, spending time with your family, or even serving others, it is good to *do* the things that energize and delight us. But even here we must be careful that we do not allow these activities to become the sources of our soul's deepest desires. We miss out on so much of what God has to offer if we allow the enemy to convince us that these experiences are the pinnacle of satisfaction.

So, the point of this devotional book was not to minimize or demonize the people, things, or experiences that make our lives sweet. However, I do hope you see that while these things may bring us some measure of joy, none of them are to be the well to which we run daily for our soul's sustenance. Jesus alone can satisfy our souls. He does it consistently, freely, splendidly, and willingly. I hope you are completely convinced of these truths after 31 days of a steady diet of the bread of life.

From Here on Out

So how do you continue to feed your soul with the bread of life from this day on? It is not nearly as difficult as you may think.

If you have filled a 4x6 photo album with index cards bearing meaty scriptures, you already have at your disposal a soul-satisfying menu from which to dine. Those biblical truths never expire or become tiresome dishes. I encourage you to continue to feed your hungry soul these basic and foundational truths.

But I am sure you will also want to savor new delights from God's Word. So let me share with you how I go about finding tasty morsels from the Bible to feast upon.

- As I listen to sermons, teaching messages, or even Christian radio, I anticipate God feeding my soul from His Word. When I hear the speaker mention a Bible passage that particularly speaks to a specific soul hunger I have been experiencing, I simply make note of the passage so I can look it up again later. Often I end by adding one or more of those verses to my scripture meditation album.

- I try to read through the Bible each year using a Daily Bible version. I prefer to read a little from the Old Testament, New Testament, Psalms, and Proverbs each day. As I read, I anticipate God feeding my current soul desires. I'll admit, I do not necessarily pull out a particularly tasty truth to add to my meditation album every day, but I do add to it from my daily readings consistently enough. Every day God feeds me through the reading of His Word, but sometimes it is through a historical account of His activity, the story of someone else's relationship with Him, or challenging commands. I may not find a succinct verse to record in my meditation book on those days, but I have been fed.

- As I am studying the Bible through small group or personal Bible studies, I watch for scriptures that speak to my needs. I try to find a balance of scriptures that feed my soul but also encourage, convict and challenge me.

- Sometimes I simply have to ask someone else for advice on finding a scripture from God's Word that speaks to a particular need. Just like sharing a sweet dessert at a favorite restaurant, sharing scriptures among friends is an especially satisfying way to experience the goodness of God.

- I attempt to memorize every passage I add to my album. The goal of memorization, of course, is a sweet incentive to keep the scriptures I choose short and focused. I have simply found that my truest and most dedicated meditation takes place in my attempts to memorize. I know it's a daunting suggestion, but I highly recommend you try to memorize at least one soul-satisfying Bible verse every two weeks.

There is something very intimate and significant about finding a soul-satisfying scripture in God's Word for yourself, writing it down, adding it to your personal scripture meditation album, and hiding it in your heart through memorization. Every time I add a verse to my album, I feel that God has intentionally and compassionately fed me from His very hand. And indeed I think He has.

I want to conclude this journey we have shared with one final word of encouragement. Friend, I assure you there has been nothing that has changed my life more, grown me up more or fed my starving soul more than meditating on the bread of life. I have studied the Bible diligently and rather thoroughly for well over 20 years. I have read through the Bible completely a number of times. And I have listened to more sermons and scripture lessons than the average person, since I am married to a pastor. These are all worthwhile and beneficial spiritual disciplines, and I highly recommend reading, studying, and hearing the Word of God. But the single thing that I would attribute with satisfying my soul, and even supplying enough sustenance for me to share with others, is meditating on and memorizing scripture. I am convinced that eating the bread of life through these two disciplines is a bona fide game changer. I implore you to take your permanent seat at the King's table and join me for the feast. May you say,

Thy words were found and I ate them,
And Thy words became for me a joy
and the delight of my heart...
(Jeremiah 15:16a)

How to Begin a Soul-Satisfying Relationship with Jesus, the Bread of Life

If you would like for Jesus to satisfy the hungers of your soul, you must first invite Him to work in your life. You must give Him permission to move into your heart, where His greatest work takes place, and to become the Lord of your life.

Unfortunately, one very big thing stands in the way of God working in your life: your sin. While God created the world perfectly so He could have sweet fellowship with us, we messed up God's plan by going our own way. When we live independently of God and do things contrary to His perfect standard of right and wrong, we sin. We miss the mark.

The Bible tells us we *all* have sinned.

For all have sinned and fall short of the glory of God. (Romans 3:23)

Therefore, we all owe the penalty for sin, which is death.

For the wages of sin is death... (Romans 6:23a)

You might think, "But I'm not dead. I haven't died because of my sin." But in fact, you have suffered the consequences of your sin. You see, because of our sin, we are separated from our God. If you are separated from God, the source of all life, you are not fully alive.

The good news is that Jesus has taken care of our sin problem. He paid the penalty for our sins so we do not have to. Jesus died for our sins on the cross, and then He conquered sin and death by rising from the grave. We have a risen Savior who lives!

But God demonstrates His own love toward us, in that while we were yet sinners, Christ died for us.
(Romans 5:8)

For God so loved the world,
that He gave His only begotten Son,
that whoever believes in Him should not perish,
but have eternal life.
For God did not send the Son into the world
to judge the world, but that the world should be
saved through Him.
(John 3:16-17)

That is why you may have heard people say they have been saved. Or maybe someone has asked you if you have been saved. My bet is that you did not necessarily know you *needed* to be saved or *why* you would need to be saved. But you probably knew you longed to be satisfied. You may have felt the hunger pangs of an unsatisfied soul even if you did not understand that you were separated from God by your sin.

But the only One who can truly satisfy your soul is Jesus. And He can only do that through a living and vibrant relationship with you. Plus, He knows that the greatest need of your soul is a Savior, One who can save you from the penalty of your sin and promise you eternal life with your Creator. Still,

He will not force Himself on you. He has died for your sins, but you have to acknowledge that gift and ask Him to move into your life as your master if you want to know Him personally.

Would you like to do that?

The Bible says that if we believe in our hearts that Jesus died on the cross for our sins, we believe that three days later God raised Him from the dead, and we confess Jesus to be our Lord with our mouths, we will be saved.

...if you confess with your mouth Jesus as Lord,
and believe in your hearts that God raised Him from the dead,
you shall be saved;
for with the heart man believes, resulting in righteousness,
and with the mouth he confesses, resulting in salvation.
(Romans 10:9-10)

If you have never accepted God's free gift of salvation through Jesus Christ, I encourage you to do that today. You can trust Jesus to be your Savior and your Lord by saying a heartfelt and sincere prayer similar to this one:

Dear God,

I want You to work in my life. I admit I am a sinner and have been living independently of You. Please forgive me. Thank you for allowing Jesus to die for my sins. I know He has risen and conquered death for me. I invite You to be the Lord of my life and begin a new work in me. Thank you for coming into my life. In Jesus' name, amen.

If you chose to pray this prayer or a similar one today, welcome to the family of God! I encourage you to share this decision with someone immediately, preferably a believer in Jesus Christ who can give you more information about Jesus and how to grow in your relationship with Him. I am sure you have many questions about Jesus, what He did for you on the cross, your new relationship with Him, and the Bible. I could not possibly answer all of those questions here. Plus, you will find that you will spend the rest of your life growing in that knowledge.

The Bible tells us that when we accept Jesus as our Savior and Lord, the Holy Spirit moves into our lives to help us grow in Christlikeness. He will help you understand the Bible, hear from Him, forsake any treasured sins, and obey His commands. The process will be gradual, but you will begin to notice changes in your life. Before, you may have noticed God at work around you. Now He will be at work in you as well. And you will find yourself satisfied as never before.

If you prayed to ask Jesus into your life as your Savior and Lord, I'd love to know about it. Or if you have benefitted from this devotional guide in any way, it would do my heart good to hear from you. Please e-mail me at kay@kayharms.com. I also invite you to visit me at my blog:

www.offthebeatenpathministries.com

About the Author

Kay Harms loves teaching women how to apply the ancient words of the Bible to their modern lives. She is the author of two Bible studies: *The View from My Front Porch*, which explores how our worldviews are most commonly formed and shows women why and how to view the world from God's perspective, and *Satisfied…at Last!*, which teaches women to satisfy their hungry souls by feasting on the bread of life.

Raised in Georgia, Kay has followed her husband James to Arizona, where he tends to a local flock of believers and she concentrates on their two children and home. Kay also serves as a mentor mom for a local MOPS chapter, leads the women's ministry at her church, speaks at women's conferences and teaches weekly Bible studies.